# MYSTERY!

Alleluia!
Janis

# MYSTERY!

by

Janis Walker

Pallium Press

Scripture quotations marked BCP are from The Book of Common Prayer, 1789, 1979.

Scripture quotations marked NRSV are from The New Revised Standard Version, copyright © 1989, Division of Christian education of the National Council of the Churches of Christ in the United States of America. Reprinted by Permission.

Scripture quotations marked KJV are from The King James Version of the bible.

Every effort has been made to insure accuracy of text and quotations, and any errors or omissions brought to our attention will be corrected in future editions.

FIRST PRINTING 2013

Pallium Press, P.O. Box 60910, Palo Alto, CA 94306-0910
We regret that Pallium Press cannot accept or return unsolicited manuscripts.

Check for new titles by Janis Walker at
www.palliumpress.com

Pallium Press books are available at
www.Amazon.com, www.BarnesandNoble.com,
or at your favorite local bookstore.

front cover photo: Terry Walker - detail of the Trinity window, Church of the Nativity, Menlo Park, California

back cover photos: Terry Walker - San Francisco and Giverny, France
cover design: Janis Walker

Printed in the United States of America.

ISBN 978-0-9826883-4-2                    PP2013-2

in loving memory of

Fr. Jerry McCourt, S.J.

Brother Lawrence Thoo, S.J.

Fr. Joseph Logan, S.J.

They lived out the "Suspice" prayer of
St. Ignatius of Loyola.

"Take, Lord, and receive all my liberty,
my memory, my understanding,
and my entire will,
All I have and call my own.

You have given all to me.
To you, Lord, I return it.

Everything is yours; do with it what you will.
Give me only your love and your grace,
that is enough for me."

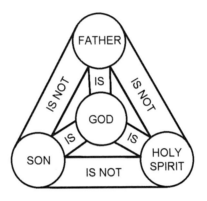

English translation of Trinity Window
on front cover

Trinity Window detail from
The Church of the Nativity
Menlo Park, CA
circa 1872

Acknowledgements

Thank you to my husband Terry,
my son Christopher,
and all whose holy lives show forth
the mystery of God's love.

A.M.D.G.

21 April 2013
Fourth Sunday of Easter
Good Shepherd Sunday

Part I   Holy Trinity Sunday, June 14, 1992

One summer morning in 1992, when I was an Episcopalian, I preached on Holy Trinity Sunday. This is the text for the homily.

In the Name of Father, and of the Son, and of the Holy Spirit.  Amen.

Today is Trinity Sunday, a glorious day in the life of the Church.  We have followed our Lord through His Passion, His death on the Cross for our salvation, His mighty Resurrection and His glorious Ascension.  Last Sunday, we celebrated the Feast of Pentecost, the coming of the promised Holy Spirit.

Trinity Sunday is a time to recall the very basic truth that One God exists in Three Persons. We'll have a look at the history behind the doctrine of the Trinity and consider some very simple examples in everyday life of how three can be one.  Finally, we'll see how all this applies to our own lives.

First of all, the mystery of the Trinity.  How can three be one?

Shelley, a friend in the parish, and I discovered that one of the things we have in common, is a love for the old Nancy Drew mystery stories.  We like the really old ones, which were published back in the 1930's and 1940's.

Nancy Drew is an intrepid young detective who lives in River Heights with her father, Carson Drew, a prominent attorney. Since the death of Nancy's mother, the family has been cared for by a devoted housekeeper named Hannah Gruen. No matter how challenging the mystery, Nancy, with the help of her chums, Bess and George, always solves it!

Shelley is a very mature young woman and perhaps has outgrown Nancy Drew. In my case, I'm not so sure!

During my years in the seminary, after studying heavy-duty subjects such as moral theology and medical ethics, I liked to relax for a little while in the evenings by reading something lighter, like Nancy Drew or the <u>Anne of Green Gables</u> books, while consuming Junior Mints!

I'm not sure even Nancy Drew could solve the mystery of the Trinity. How can God be One and yet Three at the same time?

The early Church struggled with this also. After our Lord returned to his Father and our Father in heaven, the brand-new Church was faced with spelling out its beliefs. It became very important to spell out the belief in the Holy Trinity.

The reason it was so important was that the Church was being infiltrated by a heresy called Arianism, so named (I'm sad to say) for a priest named Arius. Back then, as now, the Church was more often attacked from within than from without.

What Arius did was to deny that Jesus Christ was the divine Son of God. His Bishop, Alexander, was pretty upset by this and condemned Arius.

Well, Arius did not take the hint, but continued willfully to propagate this error. All of this was taking place in the fourth century.

People were getting really bent out of shape by this, so the Emperor Constantine called for a big Church Council at Nicea in 325 A.D. This is where we get the Nicene Creed, which we will recite in a little while. This creed came into being to defend orthodoxy, which means "right belief" as opposed to heresy.

In the Nicene Creed, we state that Jesus was of one Being with the Father. The Greek word was "homoousion," meaning "of one substance."

We also state that "We believe in the Holy Spirit, the Lord, the giver of life, who proceeds from the Father and the Son." Those words "and the Son" (also called the "Filioque") have quite a history behind them too.

3

What we need to remember is that when we say these words, they did not come easily. Those who went before us labored to preserve the correct expression of our faith.

No matter how much we study, we still come back to the conclusion that the Holy Trinity is a mystery. Not in the sense of a Nancy Drew mystery which always gets solved, but in the sense of something that is simply above reason, yet not contrary to it.

Fortunately, we don't have to understand everything in order to pray! I like to think of the old Vicar in Elizabeth Goudge's novel, <u>The Scent of Water</u>. He had served, it seemed forever, in the slums of East London. He was old and shabby and shy. And when he came to tea, he mumbled and dropped his cake on the carpet. The little girl recounting the story tells of a conversation in the garden with the old Vicar. He said to her, "My dear ... your God is a trinity. There are three necessary prayers and they have three words each. They are these, 'Lord, have mercy. Thee I adore. Into thy hands.' Not difficult to remember. If in times of distress you hold to these you will do well."

Let's consider some everyday illustrations of how three can be one. One of the oldest examples, fun to do in children's homilies, is, of course, that of water -- $H_2O$. Water is still water -- the same substance --

whether it's in liquid form, or frozen into ice cubes, or put in a teakettle and boiled off as steam. It's still the same substance -- H2O.

Another example is that of a rose. Anne Delaney, S.F.O., a sacred music composer, wrote a beautiful song, "The Rose," which is on her album "Wool on the Lamb."

As Anne wrote, the "... color, the perfume, and the beauty of the rose, do not make three roses, but one." Anne, in her song, referred also to the example of the human person.

You have a body, a spirit, and a soul (1 Thessalonians 5, 23). And yet you are ONE person.

St. Augustine, who wrote numerous books on the Trinity, also used the analogy of the human mind in its being, its knowing, and its willing.

We've looked at a bit of the history behind the doctrine of the Trinity and at a few simple illustrations. How in the world can this apply to us?

Let's recall the Lessons, the Canticle, and the Gospel for today. I felt, from the passage in Isaiah, the Canticle, and the reading from Revelation that truly a door into heaven had been opened to us. We were given glimpses into the heavenly kingdom, and then the Gospel brought us back to earth. Let's look to these passages for clues in relating to God - as Father, Son, and Holy Spirit.

What we see in all these passages is that God is HOLY.  In the visions recorded both in Isaiah and in Revelation, the celestial creatures cry out  "Holy, holy, holy is the LORD God of hosts; the whole earth is full of his glory (Isaiah 6, 3 NRSV)."  I know of no other attribute of God repeated three times.

Isaiah had a dazzling vision of the Lord on His throne and the winged seraphim.  Isaiah was overcome by a sense of his own sinfulness.  Always this is the case.  Even the tiniest glimpse of the holiness of God produces in us a sense of our own sinfulness.

In Isaiah's case, the winged creature took a burning coal from the altar, touched Isaiah's lips, and said,  "Now that this has touched your lips, your guilt has departed and your sin is blotted out (Isaiah 6, 7b NRSV)."

Isaiah, thus purified, was ready to be sent out on his mission.  In our own case, it is the shed blood of Jesus, the Lamb of God, that takes away our sins.

The great composer, Handel, told how he came to write the stirring "Hallelujah Chorus." "… I did think I did see all heaven before me, and the great God himself ( Handel's Messiah: A Devotional

Commentary, page 89, by Joseph E. McCabe)." But most of us don't have these visions. I don't.

So how can we relate to this? How can this majestic God, who "alone has immortality and dwells in unapproachable light (Eucharistic Prayer D from The Book of Common Prayer)" be our Father?

So many people have great difficulty in relating to God as Father because of their earthly fathers. You may say, "No one really wanted me. I was an 'accident.' " That's just not so.

God the Father called your life into existence. You may have been a surprise to your earthly parents, but you were no surprise to God. You most definitely were not an "accident."

God the Father wanted you in this world and He called you into being. Maybe your parents did not know how to love you or to care for you, but God the Father loves you with a perfect love. He can heal all those old hurts and use your life in a remarkable way.

Do not say "I am too young." Remember the young prophet, Jeremiah, who protested that he was a mere boy who did not know how to speak. The Lord said to Jeremiah, "Do not say, 'I am only a boy'; for you shall go out to all to whom I send you, and you shall speak whatever I command you. Do not be afraid of them, for I am with you to deliver you, says the LORD (Jeremiah 1, 7-8 NRSV)."

Remember the young Jewish teenage girl, Mary, chosen by God to be the mother of Jesus. The angel Gabriel came to Mary and said, "Hail, thou that art highly favored, the Lord is with thee: blessed art thou among women (Luke 1:28 KJV)."

Do not say, "It is too late. I am too old." Remember Moses. He was eighty years old when God appeared to him in the burning bush and told him of his mission to free the people of Israel.

Remember Abraham and Sarah. When Abraham was 99 years old and Sarah was a mere 89, God came on the scene and said, in effect, "Guess what! You two are going to have a baby."

Scripture records that "… Abraham fell on his face and laughed, and said to himself, 'Can a child be born to a man who is a hundred years old? Can Sarah, who is ninety years old, bear a child (Genesis 17, 17 NRSV)?'" God said to Abraham, "… your wife Sarah shall bear you a son, and you shall name him Isaac. I will establish my covenant with him as an everlasting covenant … (Genesis 17, 19 NRSV)."

Sarah laughed also, but Isaac was born right on God's schedule. With God it's never too late. All things are possible with God!

Because God is our Father, that makes Jesus our BROTHER! We call Him Lord and Savior and rightly so, but He is also our Brother.

Jesus was perfectly human as well as perfectly divine. The pure and spotless Lamb of God who takes away our sins was also the weary and thirsty young Jewish man who sat beside Jacob's well and asked for a drink of water.

As the writer to the Hebrews says, Jesus had to become like us "… in every respect, so that he might be a merciful and faithful high priest in the service of God, to make a sacrifice of atonement for the sins of the people. Because he himself was tested by what he suffered, he is able to help those who are tested (Hebrews 2:17-18 NRSV)."

Especially in John's Gospel, we notice Jesus saying over and over, "… the Son can do nothing of his own, but only what he sees the Father doing; for whatever the Father does, the Son does likewise (John 5, 19 NRSV)."

Jesus stated, "… I seek to do not my own will but the will of him who sent me (John 5, 30c NRSV)" and "… I have come down from heaven, not to do my own will, but the will of him who sent me (John 6, 38 NRSV)." So, if you want to know what God the Father is like, look at Jesus.

9

Before the crucifixion, Jesus told his followers of the promised Holy Spirit. The Holy Spirit is the One who will lead us and guide us into all truth.

The same Holy Spirit who raised Jesus from the dead lives in us who believe. And, as we prepare for Eucharist, we thank God that He will send the Holy Spirit upon the bread and wine to be for us the Body and Blood of our Lord Jesus Christ.

"The grace of our Lord Jesus Christ, the love of God, and the communion of the Holy Spirit, be with all of you (2 Corinthians 13, 13 NRSV). Amen.

Part II   Brief personal reflections

ONE GOD, ONE CHURCH, ONE LOVE


A. ONE GOD, Three Persons

Once, when I was agonizing over the eternal problem of free will and human suffering, I asked the Lord,  "How do YOU bear it?"

The "answer" that seemed to come to me was, "We live in community: Father, Son, and Holy Spirit."


B. ONE CHURCH

A very holy man of God was the Rector of the Episcopal Church we attended in Texas before moving to California.  I remember his speaking of the One, Holy, Catholic, Apostolic Church as the Church Militant, The Church Expectant, and the Church Triumphant.

The Church Militant is where we are now on earth.  The Church Expectant is being purified and prepared.  The Church Triumphant is what we all long for, HEAVEN!

11

C. ONE LOVE

GOD IS LOVE!

"Beloved, let us love one another, because love is from God; everyone who loves is born of God and knows God. Whoever does not love does not know God, for God is love. God's love was revealed among us in this way: God sent his only Son into the world so that we might live through him. In this is love, not that we loved God but that he loved us and sent his Son to be the atoning sacrifice for our sins. Beloved, since God loved us so much, we also ought to love one another. No one has ever seen God; if we love one another, God lives in us, and his love is perfected in us (1 John 4, 7-12 NRSV)."

Albino Luciani, Cardinal of Venice, was elected Pope on August 26, 1978. The new Pope chose the name John Paul. His book, Illustrissimi, published in 1976, was a collection of "letters" he wrote to all sorts of people, including saints and authors.

In his letter to Sainte Thérèse of Lisieux, the "Little Flower," Cardinal Luciani wrote of love in the chapter entitled "Joy, Exquisite Charity." Quoting Archbishop Perini, he noted that there are not many loves, but "only one."

Pope John Paul's angelus address of September 24, 1978, was entitled "Love Can Do Everything." It is reprinted in the book, The Smiling Pope, The Life and Teaching of John Paul I, by Raymond and Lauretta Seabeck.

The very first encyclical of Pope Benedict XVI was Deus Caritas Est (God is Love). The Pope wrote, "In a world where the name of God is sometimes associated with vengeance or even a duty of hatred and violence, this message is both timely and significant ... I wish to speak of the love which God lavishes upon us and which we in turn must share with others."

The Pope addressed the language problem and, of course, the various Greek words for love. This beautiful letter, God is Love, is available to be read online as well as in a printed book form.

N.B. Please read about the Holy Trinity in the Catechism of the Catholic Church, 2nd Edition. You may also read the Catechism and papal encyclicals online.

Part III  THE MYSTERY FUDGE

Francis, our gentle, golden Gospel Cat, made a number of trips to the vet hospital because he was always getting into adventures.  Some were very scary, as in the summer when I was serving in Clinical Pastoral Education at the people hospital and Francis had to have surgery, simple but necessary, at the animal hospital.

The vet looked bewildered and said,  "This just does not happen." That was after Francis made several truly remarkable recoveries.  With a shake of the head, the vet said,  "There goes another of his lives."

Little did the vet know that I had, in desperation, phoned the Poor Clares at the Immaculate Heart Monastery to implore the Sisters please to pray for Francis! The Sisters were very kind and understanding; they were used to me.

So when I made this "mystery" fudge for the vet hospital staff,  Kristen, one of the vet techs, announced,  "I know what the mystery ingredient is!" That was when I let the butterscotch pieces  retain a bit of their own identity and not to melt completely with the semi-sweet chocolate pieces.

15

Three ingredients for one delicious fudge!

Sweetened condensed milk (14 ounce can or the black and white cow bottle from Trader Joe's)

18 ounces of chocolate chips – can also be 12 ounces of chocolate chips and 6 ounces of another flavor, such as cinnamon, mint, peanut butter, or butterscotch or whatever.  Here is your chance to experiment!

1 teaspoon pure vanilla extract (or another flavor)

This is how I make it.  I put the condensed milk and the candy pieces in an 8-cup microwave-safe glass bowl and microwave two minutes on high. (Or you could heat it in a saucepan over low to medium heat, stirring constantly,  until the chocolate chips melt).  Then I mix it with a spoon, add the vanilla, and put it into a buttered pan.  Be sure and have the pan or whatever you want to put it in ready, because the fudge will start to harden really fast.  At this point, I pop it into the fridge.  If you are making it for a holiday, be sure and see Rachael Ray's Fudge Wreath recipe (available online).

There are endless variations you can try!  On Valentine's Day, you could pour it into a heart pan.  If you do make Rachael's holiday wreath, it is good to put an 8 inch or 9 inch parchment liner in the round cake pan before you add the fudge. Sur La Table sells these and they really come in handy. Or, you can cut out your own circles from a roll of parchment paper. Be sure and butter the sides of the pan even though you will add the parchment circle. It will help when you transfer the wreath to a plate. Then you can leave it plain or add jelly beans on top if it is an Easter wreath.

Janis Walker is the author of <u>Alleluia! A Gospel Diary</u>, <u>A Trip to Grace</u>, and <u>Shepherds</u>. She received her M.A. Theology degree from St. Patrick's Seminary in 1991. Janis was received into the Roman Catholic Church on May 13, 1998, in Rossi Chapel at the Jesuit Retreat Center, in a Chrism Mass for Christian Unity. Janis and her family are enjoying the beautiful springtime in California in between writing, swimming, editing, flying remote control gliders, designing integrated circuits, and making fudge.